An Insightful Journal for the Spiritual Journey

333

ONENESS

©2020 by Roni Hopkins
All rights reserved.
ISBN: 978-1-7349035-1-5

JOURNALS OF REALIZATION

"The only truth one could ever die for is the truth they themselves have become"

Roni Hopkins is the creator of *Journals of Realization,* which are a collection of unique journals that specialize in spirituality and consciousness. She has traveled the world, connecting with all walks of life and lives her purpose dedicated to assisting others on their journey. The creation of these journals reflect those experiences and bring a level of universal insight to ones own spiritual path. Journals of Realization encourages you to discover and express your truth, wisdom and ever evolving awareness throughout the pages and beyond them through our virtual discussions.

Every path reveals its truth within you.

www.RoniHopkins.com

PREFACE

Oneness is not a belief or a religion that beckons the truths to be told and passed down for centuries. It is not a set of rules or sects that one would have to follow.

This idea of Oneness

What does it mean to a mind that naturally perceives from a perspective of individuality and singularity to everything that it encounters?

It is not easy to comprehend that an idea of such vastness can even exist and that somehow you are a part of it, as it.

Oneness can only be experienced from a perspective of the One itself.

It shifts the *realness* of our reality and life flows from uncharted perceptions of what is possible. Creation is constantly creating between multiple realities of our existence and we find ourselves a part of it All.

Everything is new and every moment holds lifetimes in its seconds.

Oneness unveils itself in many forms and ways to each and every single one of us.

I am one.

Possesses more existence in those three words than all the lives ever lived

As you journey to discover more of yourself and the spiritual nature of all, the concept of oneness will expand your existence beyond the I , the me, and the you.

This is your Spiritual Journey

From Pen to Paper

Your Thoughts

Your Experiences

Your Realizations

"Stillness of the body and silence of the mind unlocks the door, from there you are able to observe from a perspective of Aloneness"

In stillness and aloneness the connection of yourself and with All becomes boundless.

That is the journey of meditation. It is discovering the eternal within.

In our states of true vulnerability we are open to allowing the eternal nature of All to freely flow.

For the wind to whisper through every inhale and exhale

For the sun to shine within you at the rise of a day

For the moon to illuminate its glow within your soul

For the stars to shine through the deepest parts of darkness

The pureness and simplicity of All creation becomes this immeasurable force within you.

6

14

" We come from an existence of infinite nature to be birthed in a state where we are unaware of it all"

We forget that our oneness is the only real existence there is and we do not lack anything we feel we need to seek for

We come here completely unaware of the awareness of it all

When we begin to discover as though they are ancient secrets lost in time, life takes on a new meaning to live.

" Your soul knows what your mind has yet to perceive and to believe is possible"

Our soul is the composition of *Oneness*.

It is your eternal compass through time. It holds all the guidance and understanding that we often feel lost from. The true fulfillment of your life and any vision you see rest in the blueprint of your soul.

It is essential to your life to understand the language it speaks, as it can lead you through the impossible and create a life that we can only dream as possible.

In between life happenings when your mind cannot give you the answers you are seeking, take a moment to be still and listen to the guidance your soul speaks.

Echoes

It beams through the darkest of spaces
And what is dark to something that only reflects light

Your truth echoes over and over

"I am that which is always and forever"
With every I, the tears fall
Until you become the always and the forever

The vastness of life bleeds through your veins
No longer restricted to this body, this way of life

You are free

In that freedom, you are no longer the victim or the prey
You are no longer the lost or the broken hearted
The fear or the sorrow

You drink from an abundance that is ever flowing with
Fulfillment and strengthening your ability to light the flame in
Others

The very breath that consumes your lungs is no longer a breath
Of survival but one that exhales life into the earth

You become the infinite

The universe that is boundless in distance and stretches beyond
Time

And just when you try to wrap your mind around what is
Happening through you

You find yourself starting from infinity to forever all over again

" You are with you beyond time and space. You are the eternal connection to that which is infinite"

We are constantly trying to make things that are finite eternal. The pain we suffer is because that is impossible to do.

Suffering is not the pain itself. Suffering is the constant state of pain which we cannot escape and much of that pain is derived from a state of not being able to let go of that which is no longer existing in the present state of now.

Throughout your life, what lies within you is the only constant that will remain with you from beginning to the end. The discovery of what lies beneath is the infinite nature that becomes the source of All that you are and beyond.

You are the eternal that last forever.

333

" Everything is created with perfect purpose and with that purpose all things exist"

There comes a point in all of our lives where we begin to sense something of deeper purpose for ourselves. Something that holds a true value to our being. We long to discover this.

To have such a level of completeness where a continual state of fulfillment actually sustains itself

That which we long for is the true nature of our existence. All things exist in this earth to reflect Oneness.

To discover pieces of life's beautiful creation outside of yourself and realizing those pieces are not lost but extensions of who you are

That is the perfect purpose of our human existence.

" You are the inevitable change. The constant nature of all that exist and expands."

The constant nature of all existence of life flows from this state of being.

Every Tree

Every Flower

Every Living Being

It all exist on the spectrum of change and so do you.

It is in your very nature much like nature to do so.

"There is a place inside all of us that mirrors the soul of the source. The oneness, the thread that connects us all together"

It reflects in the purest of moments that we often remember as unforgettable. In the laughter of a child, the smell of flower, the joy of being love.

We all share in the pureness of oneness and it illuminates to consume all that we are.

It is the difference as one watching a sunset and one experiencing the sunsetting within them.

When we are open to such a state of vulnerability where we are no longer afraid of ourselves, we will find our truest existence come alive.

A Stillness of Nothing

Darkness
Something that frighten one as a child has now become your solitude
A stillness of nothing
That radiates peace and freedom

To become everything one has to expand omnipresently
Into itself over and over again

Eternally changing
Daily Releasing
Yourself
Out to yourself

So that the continuous reflection of what you see is a new you
That is the Eternal Existence of the All

No identity to define oneself as
And no security to cling on to
Your freedom is wrapped in being nothing
Solidified not to be defined at all
But simply Everything

Limitless Being

You are always and forever
You are yesterday, today and tomorrow
You are the beginning and the end
You are birth, life and death

You have become all things to experience everything
Reduced to a continuous existence in time

And when you wake from dreaming
stepping upon the morning horizon

You find yourself expanding into

"*We live this life on earth constantly seeking to be more of who we are. You are all you ever need to be*"

Seeking anything rather its happiness, peace, love will only lead to a continuous pattern of trying to find it. Implying none of those things you are nor possess.

In your spiritual being all their lies.

Simply be.

Get in touch with that being. The abundant source of life within you.

"*I am nothing as I am everything*"

Spiritual Realization is not something we can achieve in hierarchy. It is a constant state of being that requires you to operate from multiple perspectives. Life is constantly flowing from a state of new creation and from there we also are new.

All sense of self expands beyond self and all sense of individuality merges into something far greater than what you could have ever imagined.

You are nothing as You are everything.

When the journey begins to create this from within
All becomes your reflection.

"Your day to day is not seeing yourself inadequate in your created being but discovering ways to be the fullness of who you are."

The only fault if there was ever one would be waking up each day and not living out your optimal potential. You are doing yourself a disservice if you do not do so.

Discover new ways to expand in the fullness of what you are.

Try new ways to live and move through this earth.

The joys of exploring and doing things that you have never done before will perpetuate your life into a newness that will bring a breath of fresh air to your existence.

You are more than capable in ways that are limitless.

www.ingramcontent.com/pod-product-compliance
Lightning Source LLC
Chambersburg PA
CBHW031117080526
44587CB00011B/1008